JIM LAMBIE

VICTORIA MORTON

JULIE ROBERTS

Painting Not Painting

TATE

Jim Lambie
Zobop
2003 (detail)
vinyl tape
dimensions variable
installation view, Tate St Ives
© the artist

Victoria Morton
Myself when I am Real
2002 (detail)
oil on canvas
2060 x 2050 mm
© the artist
courtesy The Modern Institute,
Glasgow

Julie Roberts
Annie Chapman
2001 (detail)
graphite on paper
470 x 380 mm
© the artist
courtesy Sean Kelly Gallery,
New York

introduction

Susan Daniel-McElroy

director, Tate St Ives

Painting Not Painting, brings together three artists whose work has an unnerving ambition that shakes our expectations of what painting or object-making should be about. In the juxtaposition of the ideas behind the works in this exhibition, Jim Lambie, Victoria Morton and Julie Roberts show how artists' ideas can be fresh, self-aware, contradictory and open-ended. Each artist is knowledgeable of art history and deploys that knowledge effectively to disturb our expectations.

Painting Not Painting includes the seventh installation of Jim Lambie's signature multi-coloured work *Zobop*. Located in the curved upper terrace and both staircases, the piece plays with our perception giving a 'head rush' at particular points of its installation where the kinks and quirks of the building's architecture shapes the visual dynamic of his piece. His installation *Prismatic Room (Instant Tan)* presents an iconoclastic clash of elements that invite a variety of responses from pure retro 'disco joy' and a mad desire to dance, to paranoid anxiety.

Julie Roberts' *Jack* series of drawings is presented in a Victorian atmosphere on a hand-painted wall decoration which depicts writhing *Convulvulous* plants. The seductive drawings of the Ripper's victims (real and suspected) have taken on the camera's ability to make beautiful the horrific. (The images were drawn from original 'scene of the crime' photographs.) This installation seduces us and then puts us in the uncomfortable position of voyeur. At the same time, it reveals something about artists' historical affinity with dark subjects. Her hand-made Hepworth wallpaper shown in Gallery 1, introduces a representational image of Hepworth making work into an abstract context by underpinning the display of the Pier Arts Centre Collection of St Ives artists. It also highlights the artist's interest in Barbara Hepworth as an inspirational role model for her and female artists in Britain generally. Through its disruption of a conventional white cube display, new thoughts are brought to bear on what can constitute an artwork.

Victoria Morton's works are unashamedly lush oil paintings packed with the richness and energy of space, colour and mark-making. The painted surface often invites our eye to 'fall into' the interior space of the painting and in some passages of paint the artist appears to have 'excavated' the painterly marks in such a way that colour appears to project from the surface. Halfway between figuration and abstraction, these works have a potent hypnotic power to engage us as we search for meaning and order in a surface which seems to expand beyond the edges of the painting and denies the possibility of identification of subject matter.

Seeing the playful, the mysterious or the unexpected can re-energise our thoughts about the language of art. In the end, it is art that provokes us to question and debate its value which keeps our interest and the language of art alive and kicking. The work of Jim Lambie, Victoria Morton and Julie Roberts reaches beyond the rigid convention of classification. Their art sets out to subvert the more usual museological approach that art historians often use to discuss the incremental development of artists, their work and their comparisons and relationships within art history.

I must thank the Hepworth Estate for giving kind permission to use an image of Barbara Hepworth to create the wallpaper design. Thanks also to Pier Arts Centre's Director Neil Firth for agreeing to the collection display and its disruption by this means.

Jim Lambie and Julie Roberts were assisted by Danny Saunders and Nickola Byrne respectively – our warm thanks to them and to the members of staff at Tate St Ives who worked hard to install *Zobop*.

We are particularly grateful to the David S Cohen Foundation for supporting the exhibition and to Tate colleagues who supported the St Ives team in its preparation.

Will Bradley's essay provides us with a fresh, enjoyable, fast and incisive 'take' on this context and the artists included in *Painting Not Painting*.

Finally I must thank all three artists for participating in this exhibition which will, I am sure, cause much debate over the coming months.

Jim Lambie
Roadie
1999 (detail)
turntable, coat hangers, glitter
dimensions variable
© the artist
courtesy The Modern Institute,
Glasgow

Victoria Morton
Winter Painting
After All Friends
Together the Friends
Turn into Flowers
1999 (detail)
oil on canvas
2000 x 2300 mm
© the artist
courtesy The Modern Institute,
Glasgow

Julie Roberts
Edvard Munch Death Mask
2001 (detail)
oil on canvas
470 x 380 mm
private collection, New York

Painting Not Painting

Will Bradley

The title of this exhibition, 'Painting Not Painting', sums up Modern art's schizophrenic inability to pin down the qualities of the medium that first brought it into being. In order to understand how it relates to Jim Lambie, Victoria Morton and Julie Roberts, it is perhaps useful to look at how Modern painting tried to understand itself.

Painting about painting, theorised by Braque among others, was an investigation into the conditions and possibilities of representation, and into the qualities of the painters' materials themselves, a journey through rocky and uncharted territory whose twin peaks, gained after great struggle, were maybe Jackson Pollock's drip paintings and Robert Ryman's white monochromes. Mondrian, an early convert, grew to think of 'subject matter' in painting as 'a hindrance' – it interfered with the viewer's apprehension of form and colour and the intellectual relationships thus expressed. Nowadays, abstract painting of all kinds is a familiar part of our culture, another 'subject matter' like anything else, and Mondrian would be stuck in a closed loop, but back then the art world was still reeling from the deadpan brilliance of Malevich's *Black Square*. By the 1960s, painting about painting meant a cool, conceptual engagement with the short but overloaded cultural history of this simple idea, and, with the help of Ad Reinhardt's own black paintings, pronounced the whole expanded field dead. In the seventies, nobody painted, at least nobody anyone remembers, because they were trampled in the eighties, when painting about painting came back with a flourish and a quick flick through the history books. Pantomime expressionism, faux-idiot savantism and other glitzy deconstructions of a forgotten and worthless version of history were served up by virtuoso showmen playing Beethoven with one hand and Elton John with the other – a rock star trip with Basquiat, Kippenberger, Salle and Schnabel, until the money ran out. In the nineties nobody painted.

Which isn't true either, not exactly, but it is true that the environment in which Lambie, Morton and Roberts started out, the art scene of the late eighties and early nineties in Glasgow, was dominated by the aesthetics and ideas of neo-conceptualism – video, text work, found objects. The German and American-led painting revival of the early eighties had had its counterpart in the New Glasgow Boys, a group of young painters whose illustrative, neo-socialist-realist style began to grate very quickly, and the backlash that followed was fierce. Formalism in general, and painting in particular, became something of a no-go area for the ambitious young artist. One exhibition, at the Centre for Contemporary Art in the mid-nineties, was even titled 'The Persistence of Painting' in recognition of the medium's apparently embattled state. This isn't to say the climate of that time was restrictive or faddish, but there weren't that many UK artists who got through 1994 without picking up a video camera. What it did provide was an acute awareness of the failures and dead-ends of the formalisms of the past, combined with a rediscovery of the possibilities offered by the Fluxus movement, the Californian performance scene of the early seventies, and the poetic conceptualism of artists like Lawrence Weiner.

The point of all this, in relation to 'Painting Not Painting', is that although the artists involved all chose, in different ways, to sidestep that prevailing trend, all of their work is marked by this critical crossover as much as by older traditions, and all of their work has an underlying complexity and engagement that marks it out from the current revival in painting and sculpture. After all, as an artist you might be noticed for the similarities between your work and work from the past, but you get remembered for the differences.

JIM LAMBIE'S clued-up iconoclasm is a perfect example. Much has been made of Lambie's rock and roll past, and many of his works are titled after more or less well-known records of the last thirty years, but that's maybe the least interesting thing about them. Reversing Duchamp's famous ideal Ready-Made, he offers something more like an ironing-board used as a Rembrandt, a smart but casual burst of junk-shop alchemy. Different to the paradoxical preciousness of, for example, Arte Povera, with its rejection of expensive traditional art materials in favour of the debris of industrialisation, Lambie's reanimation of tattered record sleeves, flea-market fashion and third-hand furniture doesn't ask to be admired for its humility or its triumph in adversity, but wants to be seen on its own terms.

Psychedelic Soul Stick
1998
bamboo, thread, wire,
mixed media
dimensions variable
© the artist
courtesy The Modern Institute,
Glasgow

Zobop has already become a signature work, albeit one whose defining characteristic is that it's different every time. As with Lambie's *Psychedelicsoulsticks*, or his ongoing series of works made by collaging thousands of eyes cut from magazine photographs onto posters of rock stars, the instant impact belies the meticulous and labour intensive work of production. Formed by the outline of the floor, highlighting and amplifying asymmetries and imperfections, *Zobop* is also one of very few contemporary works to escape, or at least overpower, the restrictions of the white-cube aesthetic. Obvious ancestors – Carl Andre's walk-on floor pieces, Bridget Riley's op-art stripe paintings, Sol LeWitt's instruction drawings – seem to sink under their own weight and disappear over one of *Zobop*'s illusory perpendicular cliffs.

Lambie's work doesn't define itself against its predecessors, but draws its energy from an easy acknowledgement that art can both affect everyday experience and be shaped by it. It's a mirror-image union of art and life, not Warhol's soup cans, Pollock in a jazz club or Joseph Beuys planting trees, but a deliberate refusal to recognise the value-systems that make those things meaningful. Lambie mobilises a decentred view of art history – a personal vocabulary of materials and techniques combined with an astute but heretical awareness of the past – deployed with such simplicity and confident intelligence it feels like part of a common culture that was there all along. Many well-revered artists spent years of their lives justifying their decision to make black squares, or mirror cubes, or screenprinted filmstars, but rather than standing on the shoulders of the giants of the past, Lambie simply leapfrogs them, as if to say, why wait? If there's any relationship between his art and rock and roll, it's that he makes formal questions in sculpture seem as live and satisfying as the Modern Lovers playing *Pablo Picasso*, Television doing *Venus de Milo*, or Bowie's *Andy Warhol*.

Zobop
2003 (detail)
vinyl tape
dimensions variable
installation view, Tate St Ives
© the artist

JIM LAMBIE

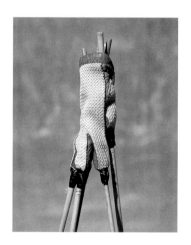

Prismatic Room (Instant Tan)
2003 (detail)
mixed media
dimensions variable
installation views, Tate St Ives
© the artist

VICTORIA MORTON'S primary interest has always been in the representational space of the painted canvas. From her earliest artschool skyscapes, through a period of spraygun experiments that recalled John Latham's *One Second Paintings*, scattering droplets of paint like distant galaxies over vistas of infinite depth, and a later engagement with layered gestural techniques, a kind of cooled down De Kooning, Morton assembled a repertoire of techniques and imagery that caught fire, so to speak, with her 1996 painting *Dirty Burning*. An intense flurry of abstract marks, a swirling shower of sparks and smoke, *Dirty Burning* was the bonfire on which she burnt her influences and signalled a new beginning.

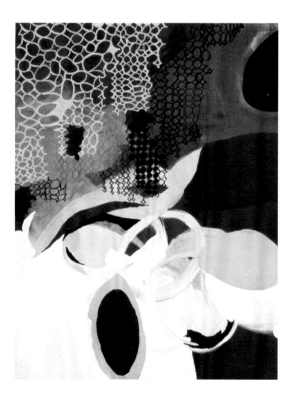

Gilt Mint
1998
oil on canvas
400 x 300 mm
© the artist
courtesy The Modern Institute,
Glasgow

Everyday Friction
2000
oil on canvas
1800 x 1600 mm
© the artist
courtesy The Modern Institute,
Glasgow

Ever since, her time has been spent discovering how a painting should be formed here and now. The experience of looking at one of Morton's paintings often begins with a dizzying rush, a vertiginous feeling of depth and motion that makes you acutely aware of the process of looking and seeing, of the decisions needed to order the pictorial elements in time and space and the subconscious tricks your brain employs to try and resolve the unknown into a familiar shape, but she uses this physiology both ways, at times denying it with dense, flat, canvases that seem to suck light inwards. The goal isn't beauty, or balance, or the harmonious combination of colour and form, but a kind of precision: a visual description of a process of reflection. It's an exact uncertainty, an unnameable emotion, scientific Romance. An unsolvable mystery illuminated in perfect detail.

Unlike traditional easel painting, where the artist looks beyond the canvas at the subject to be drawn from life, or Modernist abstraction where the artist views the canvas as an object, a prop in a performance or a surface to be covered, Morton seems to look behind the picture plane, to work inside the hallucinatory virtual space of representation. Each brushstroke, though often almost flat, seems like one aspect of a three-dimensional form, one view of a hologram, and in this sense the work presents an absolutely contemporary idea of space and vision. You can imagine her painting with a Walkman on (she also makes installation works where light and sound are the main components), immersed in a kind of low-tech virtual reality. In some of her newest works, the canvases are presented freestanding, hinged like Renaissance screens – a technique from a time when lifelike oil painting really was the new technology – the better both to surround the viewer and to demonstrate, Wizard of Oz-like, the nature of the illusion.

The plastic nature of reality, guessed at by the Surrealists and made mystical by the psychedelic visionaries of the sixties, is an accepted fact in the digital age, and Morton uses painting as a tool to explore this new world as much as she explores the legacy of painting from Lascaux through Giotto, Ernst, O'Keefe and Hockney among many others. Scenes from the history of images melt and flow together with a dreamlike intensity. In Morton's practice, the art of the past exists not as tradition but as immediate fact, not as context but as an environmental condition, a heat-haze or a snowfall that leads to a new understanding of the landscape.

Morton's work is set apart from much contemporary painting by the way it refuses to accept that the medium can no longer develop within its own parameters. Contemporary artists tend to use the canvas either as a glorified diary, a graffiti artist's scrapbook, a medium for illustration, or an ironic signifier of Modernist art history. Morton demonstrates that painting's potential for image-making and experimentation remains as strong as ever.

Winter Painting
After All Friends
Together the Friends
Turn into Flowers
1999
oil on canvas
2000 x 2300 mm
© the artist
courtesy The Modern Institute,
Glasgow

overleaf

Night Geometry
2002 (diptych)
oil on canvas
each 2600 x 2050 mm
© the artist
courtesy The Modern Institute,
Glasgow

The Temples
2002 (diptych)
oil on canvas
2050 x 700 mm, 2050 x 800 mm
© the artist
courtesy The Modern Institute, Glasgow

Sedate Saturate
2002
oil on canvas
250 x 205 mm
© the artist
courtesy The Modern Institute, Glasgow

Stag
2002
oil on canvas
450 x 500 mm
© the artist
courtesy The Modern Institute, Glasgow

Myself when I am Real
2002
oil on canvas
2600 x 2050 mm
© the artist
courtesy The Modern Institute, Glasgow

It has often been said that JULIE ROBERTS' subject is the human body, specifically the way the female body has historically been represented in painting. The history of painting is a story of money, power, and institutionalised male dominance, and Julie Roberts uses her own paintings as a means to critique an often unthinking acceptance of this one-sided worldview. Bringing an unseen and unrepresented social background into the frame, she picks out loaded details and uncovers significance in the most marginal, overlooked elements. These fragments are depicted with all of the seductive, hyperreal intensity that oil colour was first celebrated for, a realism compounded from Ingres and Chuck Close, then set floating against flat monochromatic grounds. This way, despite the almost luminous detail, you can't forget you're looking only at paint, and the construction of painted reality becomes the explicit subject.

Roberts builds up meaning in a network of relationships between paintings that extends across her whole body of work, apparently innocent images taking on new overtones as they echo more sinister set-ups. One recurring theme, a simple enough study, is that of furniture, mostly tables and chairs, but as the work develops connections form that describe complex and inescapable underlying power structures. A chair implies a way of sitting, and with it a whole way of being. Roberts tracks such unspoken constraints across centuries of culture. An image of a chair designed to position women's bodies during gynaecological examination is echoed by a painting of the kind of chaise longue that Manet's Olympia reclines on, while a man like Freud gets a solid wooden desk. Interactions build up between royal thrones, beds and boudoirs, nineteenth-century séances, mortuary tables, straightjackets, dolls' houses, anatomical models, operating tables, love seats, and grotesque medical instruments. Roberts paints all of these scenes empty of people, leaving the viewer to fill the space instinctively, underlining the way social roles and institutions are inscribed in our minds as well as our environment.

Recently Roberts has begun to paint the female body. To be more exact, and more in keeping with her methods, she has begun to reproduce images of the female body, representations drawn from historical sources. In 'Painting Not Painting' she shows a

Jack
installation view, Tate St Ives
© the artist
Courtesy Sean Kelly Gallery,
New York

series of eight graphite drawings of the victims of Jack the Ripper, women known only for the sad fact of their violent and untimely deaths. Though the Ripper was never caught, much of the speculation about his identity centres on his apparent knowledge of surgical procedure. Roberts' drawings – framed Victorian-style and installed against a hand-painted watercolour motif that patterns the walls, recalling the period atmosphere of a domestic interior – seem to make a connection between the anatomical studies undertaken by classical painters and their unthinkingly objectified portrayal of women, along a continuum of male violence and domination whose terminal point is the Ripper's insanity.

JULIE ROBERTS

Mary Kelly
2001
graphite on paper
© the artist
courtesy Sean Kelly Gallery,
New York

Annie Chapman
2001
graphite on paper
© the artist
courtesy Sean Kelly Gallery,
New York

Alice McKenzie
(suspected victim)
2001
graphite on paper
© the artist
courtesy Sean Kelly Gallery,
New York

Martha Tabram
(suspected victim)
2001
graphite on paper
© the artist
courtesy Sean Kelly Gallery,
New York

Jack # Martha (woman T suspected victim) 2001

Roberts' other contribution to the exhibition, a wallpaper made up of watercolour images of sculptor Barbara Hepworth at work, acts as a counterpoint to this dramatic observation. The wallpaper serves to make a link to the St Ives scene that is far from arbitrary, celebrating a reflective and open idea of art-making in quiet opposition to the restrictive ideologies that Roberts is working to expose.

A display in this wallpapered room of work by artists associated with St Ives drawn from the collection of the Pier Arts Centre in Orkney – including several of those responsible for Britain's eventual, if slightly cold and woolly, embrace of the Modernist avant garde that had already swept Europe in the first decades of the last century – completes the circuit of geographic and art historical associations suggested by this exhibition. The work of, for example, Naum Gabo, a genius who made his first, Braque-inspired sculpture in 1915, but ended up selling the Americans a watered-down version of the Russian Constructivism he'd once renounced, or Ben Nicholson, the brilliant British painter whose development of Mondrian's ideas was ultimately of little interest to the wider world – substantiates the bogosity of the mythical unbroken lineage of Modernism and adds weight to the argument presented in 'Painting Not Painting' – against rigid categorisation and incremental development, and in favour of the way that a self-aware, open-ended and wide-ranging conception of art practice can re-energise even a discipline like painting, that was ancient before Modern was invented.

JIM LAMBIE

b1964

education

1990–1994   BA (Hons) Fine Art Glasgow School of Art

forthcoming projects

2003
The Fourth Sex Fondazione Pitti Immagine, Florence, Italy (group)
Painting Not Painting Tate St Ives (group)*
Inverleith House, Edinburgh (solo)
MART, Trento, Italy (group)
The Moderns Castello di Rivoli, Turin, Italy (group)*
Objects in mirror are closer than they appear Badischer Kunstverein,
Karlsruhe, Germany (group)
Museum of Modern Art, Oxford (solo)
Tate Trienniale Tate Britain, London (group)*

solo exhibitions

2002
Artists Statement, Basel/Miami Beach Art Fair
The Breeder projects, Athens, Greece
Jim Lambie Sadie Coles HQ

2001
Jim Lambie The Modern Institute, Glasgow
Jim Lambie Anton Kern, New York
Jim Lambie Jack Hanley San Francisco

2000
Jim Lambie Konrad Fisher, Dusseldorf
Triangle Paris
Sonia Rosso Pordenone, Italy*

1999
Weird Glow Sadie Coles HQ, London
Voidoid Transmission Gallery, Glasgow*
ZOBOP The Showroom Gallery, London

1998
Ultralow video screening Carnival, Soho, London

group exhibitions

2002
VIP Kunsthalle Palazzo, Liestal, Switzerland (group)*
EU2 Stephen Friedman Gallery, London
Greyscale CMYK Tramway, Glasgow*
New Scottish National Gallery of Modern Art, Edinburgh*
Early One Morning Whitechapel Gallery, London*
Jim Jonathon Kenny Frances and Sol Stedlijk Bureau, Amsterdam
Electric Dreams Barbican Gallery, London
Hello My Name Is… Carnegie Museum of Art, Pittsburgh
Roma Roma Roma Rome, Italy
There Is A Light That Never Goes Out Galleria Sonia Rosso, Italy
My Head Is On Fire But My Heart Is Full Of Love, Charlottenbourg Museum,
Copenhagen, Denmark*

	Painted, Printed & Produced in Great Britain, Grant Selwyn Fine Art, New York
	Gale Gates et al Brooklyn, New York
	Life Is Beautiful Laing Art Gallery, Newcastle, UK
2001	*Here and Now* Dundee Contemporary Arts, Dundee*
	Between Object and Arabesque, Kunsthallen Brandts Klaedefabrik, Denmark *
	Funktional Fictional Kunsthalle zu Kiel, Germany*
	Tailsliding British council touring show*
	Silhouettes Lenbachhaus, München, Germany *
	Painting at the Edge of the World Walker Arts Center, Minneapolis*
2000	*Electric city* The Lighthouse, Glasgow
	Off the record Bucknell Art Gallery, Pennsylvania
	Raumkörper Basel Kunsthalle, Basel
	Hoxton HQ Sadie Coles, Hoxton St, London
	Parking Meters Cologne, Germany
	Heart and soul Los Angeles
	What If Moderna Museet, Stockholm
	The British Art Show 5 Edinburgh, Cardiff, Birmingham, Southampton,
	Mark Selwyn, Los Angeles
	Black Gloss Anton Kern, New York
	Dream Machines Dundee Contemporary Arts, Mapin Gallery, Sheffield,
	Camden Arts Centre, London
1999	*Mathew Higgs* @Galerie Krinzinger, Vienna
	Papermake Modern Art Inc., London
	Creeping Revolution Foksal Gallery, Warsaw
	'To be continued...' Walsall Public Projects*
	Dots and Loops MK Expositeruimte, Rotterdam
	Heart and Soul 60 Long Lane, London
	The Queen is Dead Stills Gallery, Edinburgh*
	Silk purse Waygood Gallery, Newcastle
1998	*Lovecraft* Spacex Gallery, Exeter
	All or Nothing La Friche Gallery (Triangle) Marseille France
	Slant6 Jacob Javit's Center, New York
	The Modern Institute @ Sadie Coles HQ London
	Host Tramway, Glasgow*
	Two Up Property Gallery, Glasgow
1997	*This is...These are* Norwich
	European Couples and Others, Transmission Gallery, Glasgow
1996	*The World of Ponce* Southpark, Glasgow
	Brain Mail Broad Studio 17, Cal Art's, Los Angeles
	Girls High Fruitmarket Galley, Glasgow*
	Insanestupidphatfuctpervert Cubitt St, London

Sick building Globe gallery, Copenhagen
Insanestupidphatfuctpervert Concrete Skates, Glasgow
Art for People Transmission Gallery, Glasgow
Kilt ou Double La Vigie Gallery, Nîmes

1995   *In Stereo* Transmission Gallery, Glasgow
Mary Redmond & Jim Lambie Assembly Gallery, Glasgow
Jonnie Wilkes & Jim Lambie 115 Dalriada, Glasgow

residencies
1998   Triangle Marseille, France
2000   New York Residency, Triangle (October)

commissions and awards
2000   Paul Hamlyn Foundation Award for Artists London
1998   British Council award toward residency at Triangle, Marseille
The Modern Institute 'Ultralow' commission

reviews/articles
2001   *New York Times* 14 September Roberta Smith
Flash Art May–June Sylvia Chivaratanoud
Flash Art March–April Magdelena Kroner

2000   *New york press* feb 15th Christian Viveros- Faune
The new york times feb 18th Holland Cotter
Village Voice Feb 20 Levin
Freize Papermake Neal Brown Feb

1999   *Time Out* December (review of Weird Glow)
Self service Issue No 10 (double page spread)
I.D. Issue no 187 1999 (Stuart Shave)
Circa Issue No 87 1999 (Mark Dawes)
Seven wonders of the World published by Bookworks 1999
Art and Text Issue 65 1999 Transmission Gallery (Elisabeth Mahoney)
Frieze Issue 46 April 1999 (Ross Sinclair)
Art Monthly April/May 1999 (Nicky Bird)
ZOBOP Catalogue Transmission/Showroom Gallery Rob Tufnell

1998   *Contemporary Visual Arts Urban Myths* (Rebecca Gordon Nesbitt)
1998   *Lovecraft Catalogue* Spacex Gallery
1997   *Zing Magazine* Insanestupidphatfuctpervert (Toby Webster) 1997
Newsweek Glasgow Gets Conceptual (Peter Plagens) 1997
1995   *Circa* Issue 75 1995 Jonnie Wilkes Jim Lambie (Richard Wright)

* with catalogue

VICTORIA MORTON

b1971

lives and works in Glasgow

education

1993–1995   MFA Glasgow School of Art

1989–1993   BA (Hons) Fine Art Painting Glasgow School of Art

solo exhibitions

2003   Fruitmarket Gallery, *Visions for the Future* Commission
                     (upper gallery) Edinburgh*

2002   *Night Geometry* Gavin Browns Enterprise, New York
                     Pleasure and Practice Transmission Gallery basement project 2001
                     Sadie Coles HQ London
                     Galerie Enja Wonneberger, Kiel, Germany

1999   *The Modern Institute* Glasgow
                     Decapoda The Changing Room, Stirling*

1997   *Dirty Burning* 33 Gt Sutton St, London
                     Gallery Tre Stockholm, Sweden

1996   *Out of the Web* Fringe Gallery, Castlemilk, Glasgow
                     Transmission Gallery, Glasgow
                     Pier Arts Centre, Orkney

1995   Wilkes Dalriada, Glasgow

group exhibitions

2003   *Painting Not Painting* Tate St Ives*

2002   *New* Scottish National Gallery of Modern Art, Edinburgh*
                     My Head Is On Fire But My Heart Is Full Of Love Charlottenbourg Museum,
                     Copenhagen Denmark*
                     RomaRomaRoma Rome, Italy
                     Half the World Away Hallwalls CAC, Buffalo, New York
                     Painted, Printed and Produced in Great Britain Grant Selwyn Fine Art,
                     Beverly Hills

2001   *Casino 2001* SMAK Gent, Belgium*
                     Here and Now Dundee Contemporary Arts & Aberdeen City Art Gallery, UK*
                     Studio International The Hydra Workshop, Hydra, Greece*
                     One for One Circles Project ZKM, Kalsruhe (with Elizabeth Go)
                     Pippo Lloyd Jerome, Glasgow

2000	*The Seat With the Clearest View* curated by Polly Staple
	Grey Matter Contemporary Art, Sydney
	Tecknigar Galleri Charlotte Lund, Stockholm, Sweden
	In Glass Loopholes Intermedia, Glasgow
	Surface An Turean Arts Centre, Portree, Skye
	Film Club curated by Scott Myles, Denniston, Glasgow (with Elizabeth Go)
	A Very Nice Film Club curated by David Thorpe, Vilma Gold, London
	(with Elizabeth Go)
	Grant Selwyn Fine Arts Beverly Hills
1999	*Where the Wild Roses Grow* performance Elizabeth Go *Anti War – You Take It*
	From My Heart Transmission Gallery, Glasgow*
	The Queen is Dead Stills, Edinburgh*
	Love Speed Thrills Metropolitan University (with Elizabeth Go)
1998	*Host* Tramways, Glasgow (with Elizabeth Go)
	Hardline Catalyst Arts, Belfast
	Monoprint Glasgow Print Studio
	Slant 6 Jacob Javits Centre, New York
	Intelligible Lies Talbot Rice Gallery, Edinburgh*
	Select The Crawford Arts Centre, St Andrews
1997	*You Show Me The DF Every Night You Show Me the DF* performance
	Elizabeth Go, Connected NGCA, Sunderland*
	Group Show Free Gallery, Glasgow
	Satellite City installation by Elizabeth Go *Hit 'em With That Antionette*
	Catalyst Arts Belfast
	Stepping Up 33 Gt Sutton St, London
	Evel Machines Street Net Project New York
1996	*Loaded: A Contemporary View of British Painting* Ikon Gallery, Birmingham
	Stepping Out 33 Gt Sutton St, London
	Satellite Travelling Gallery throughout Scotland*
	Insanestupidphatfuctpervert Concrete Skates, Glasgow & Cubitt St, London
	Art For People Transmission Gallery, Glasgow
1995	*30 Secs + Title* slide works from Glasgow, Los Angeles and Toronto
	Swarm Travelling Gallery throughout Scotland*
	SBC European Art Exhibition Smith Gallery, London and Paris*
	New Rose Hotel Transmission Gallery, Glasgow
1994	*New Art In Scotland* CCA Glasgow and Aberdeen City Arts Gallery*
	Modern Art Transmission Gallery, Glasgow
	In a Still Climate Newberry Gallery, Glasgow

public collections

Scottish National Gallery of Modern Art, Edinburgh
Museum of Modern Art, San Fransisco

other information

2001–present day   makes music with Son of Kong

1997–2001   0.5 lecturer in Fine Art, Duncan of Jordanstone College of Art, Dundee

1997–2001   makes music film and installation projects with the collaborative group Elizabeth Go

2001   records soundtrack with Torsten Lauschmann for *Beeline* a film by Anne-Marie Copestake

1999–2001   plays bass with Suckle recordings on *Chemikal Underground*

2001   *Express Yourself* Channel 4 Education

2000   interviews Chicks on Speed for *Trigger Tonic* a project by Anne-Marie Copestake

1999   artist in residence *Triangle* The World Trade Centre, New York

1996   artist in residence *The Fringe Gallery* Castlemilk, Glasgow

* with catalogue

JULIE ROBERTS

b1963 Flint, Wales

education

1988–90	M.F.A. Degree, Glasgow School of Art, Scotland, UK
1986–87	Postgraduate Studies, St Martins School of Art, London, UK
1980–84	HND, Wrexham School of Art, Wales, UK

residencies

2001–02	International Studio & Curatorial Program, Manhattan, New York
1995–96	The Scottish Art Council Scholar at the British School at Rome, Italy
1992	British Council Scholarship, Budapest, Hungary
1990	Pan-European Artists Exchange Programme, Budapest, Hungary Castlemilk Womanhouse, Glasgow, Scotland, UK

selected forthcoming solo exhibitions

2003	*Picturesque* Sean Kelly Gallery New York, Fall 2003*

selected solo exhibitions

2002	*Julie Roberts/johan Nobel* Galerie Andrehn Shiptjenko, Stockholm, Sweden *Broken Home* Mezzanine, Galeria Fortes Vilaca, Sae Paulo, Brazil
2001	*Town & Country* The Pier Arts Centre, Stromness, Orkney, Scotland
1999	*Heroes and Villains* Sean Kelly Gallery, New York, USA *Estate* Project Room, Galerie Wang, Oslo, Norway
1998	*Father of Creation* Project Space, Galeria Camargo Vilaca, Sao Paulo, Paco Imperiale, Rio de Janeiro, Brazil* *Recent Paintings* Galerie Ghislaine Hussenot, Paris, France
1997	*Crime of Passion* Sean Kelly Gallery, New York, USA *The Room of The Parrots* Galerie Almut Gerber, Cologne, Germany; Curated by Barbara Hofmann *The Rome Paintings* Talbot Rice Gallery, Edinburgh, Scotland*
1996	*Infanticide. Sworn-off* Olle Olsson Husset Galerie and Museum, Stockholm, Sweden, curated by Maria Lind* *Julie Roberts* Galerie Andrehn Schiptjenko, Stockholm, Sweden *Red Vine:* Artisti britannici a Roma, British Waves Festival, The British School at Rome Gallery, Italy*
1995	*Julie Roberts* Galerie Ghislaine Hussenot, Paris, France
1993	*Julie Roberts* Interim Art, London, UK

| 1992 | *Julie Roberts* Centre for Contemporary Arts, Glasgow, Scotland, UK* |

selected group exhibitions

| 2003 | *Sanctuary* Gallery of Modern Art, Glasgow, Scotland, UK |

2002	*It's Unfair* Museum De Paviljoens, Al Almer, The Netherlands
	Paralela-uma exposicao de XXV Bienal de Sae Paulo, Sae Paulo, Brasil
	New, Recent Acquisitions of Contemporary British Art Scottish National Gallery of Modern Art, Edinburgh, Scotland*
	Rotativa Galeria Fortes Vilaca, Sao Paulo, Brasil*
	New Acquisitions Indianapolis Art Museum, USA
	Interieur Galerie Andreas Grimm, Munich, Germany

2001	*Furor Scribendi, works on paper* Angles Gallery, Santa Monica, USA
	Self/Portrait National Museum & Gallery, Cardiff, Wales, UK
	Here + Now Scottish Art 1990–2001, Dundee Contemporary Art, Aberdeen Art Gallery, and venues throughout Dundee, Scotland, UK*
	Minimal Art and its Legacy Hirshhorn Museum and Sculpture Garden, Washington DC, USA
	Domestic Acts Sean Kelly Gallery, New York
	Gallery Artists-Project Space Gallery Wang, Oslo, Norway
	Contemporary Art: Hirst, Hopkins, Roberts from the collection, Scottish National Gallery of Modern Art, Edinburgh, Scotland
	Circles 4, One For One Zentrum Fur Kunst Und Medientechnologie, Karlsruhe, Germany*

2000	*Little Angels* Houldsworth Fine Art, London, UK*
	Ecosse, 45eme Salon de Montrouge, Art Contemporain Montrouge, France
	Gallery of Contemporary Art, Lisbon, Portugal*
	Blue The New Walsall Art Gallery, England, UK*
	Complete Leeds Metropolitan University Gallery, England, UK*

| 1999 | *Circa 1968* Serralves Museum of Contemporary Art, Oporto, Portugal |
| | *Scotland's Art* City Arts Centre, Edinburgh, Scotland, UK* |

| 1998 | *Nettverk-Glasgow* Museet for Samtidskunst, Oslo, Norway* |

| 1997 | *Clean and Sane* Edsvik, Sollentuna, Sweden, Galleri F15, Moss, Norway* |
| | *Date with an Artist* Northern Gallery for Contemporary Art, Sunderland, UK*, with BBC TV Programme |

1996	*Ace* The Hayward Gallery, London, England, UK
	10# Rhona Hoffman Gallery, Chicago, USA
	Satellite Scottish Arts Council Touring Gallery, Edinburgh, Scotland, UK
	Sommerlust Galerie Meile, Lucerne, Switzerland
	Pittura Castello de Rivara, Centro d'art Contemporanea, Italia*

Recent Acquisitions The Hirshhorn Museum and Sculpture Garden, Washington, DC, USA

1995   *The Persistence of Painting* Centre for Contemporary Art, Glasgow, Scotland, UK*

The British Art Show 4 Cornerhouse Gallery, Manchester, England; Scottish National Gallery of Modern Art, Edinburgh, Scotland; National Museum of Wales, Cardiff, Wales, UK*

Swarm Scottish Arts Council, Travelling Exhibition, Scotland, UK*

Pittura Immedia: Painting in the Nineties, Neue Galerie, Kunsthalle, Graz, Austria*

Scottish Autumn Julie Roberts, Douglas Gordon, Tracy MacKenna, Museum Ludwig, Budapest, Hungary*

Passion Privées Musee dart Moderne de la Ville de Paris, Paris, France

1994   *Conceptual Living* Rhizome, Amsterdam, Holland

Don't Wake Up Interim Art, London, England, UK

Riviera, Seven Artists from Scotland Oriel Mostyn, Llandudno, Wales, UK*

Choix de Bruxelles Gallery Rodolphe Janssen, Bruxelles, Belgium

Wall to Wall Southampton City Art Gallery, South Bank Centre Touring Exhibition, England, UK*

Art Oriente Object MA Galerie, Paris, France

Nature Morte Tanya Bonakdar Gallery, New York, USA

1993   *Emergenza Aprto'93* XLV Biennale Di Venezia, Italy*

Left Luggage Recontres dans UN Couloir, Hou Hanru, Paris, France; Hans Ulrich Obrist, Hamburg; St Gallen, Switzerland

Painting Invitational Barbara Gladstone Gallery, New York, USA

1992   *Transmission at City Racing* City Racing, London, England, UK

Love at First Sight The Showroom Gallery, London, England, UK

1991   *Windfall 91* Seamans Mission, Glasgow, Scotland, UK*

Speed Transmission Gallery, Glasgow, Scotland, UK

selected collections

Tate Britain, The Scottish National Gallery of Modern Art, Edinburgh, Aberdeen Art Gallery, Scotland, The Scottish Arts Council Collection, The National Museum of Wales, The Swedish Arts Council, The Hirshhorn Museum and Sculpture Garden, Washington DC, USA, Indianapolis Art Museum, USA, Serralves Museum of Contemporary Art, Oporto, Portugal and private collections throughout North America, South America, Europe and Japan.

AHRB Fellow in the Creative and Performing Arts, Glasgow School of Art, Scotland

* with catalogue

Published to accompany

the exhibition at Tate St Ives

8 February – 11 May 2003

Tate St Ives
Porthmeor Beach
St Ives
Cornwall TR26 1TG
www.tate.org.uk

ISBN 1 85437 483 4

a catalogue record for this publication is
available from the British Library

editor   Susan Daniel-McElroy

design   Groundwork, Skipton

photos   (at St Ives) Woodley & Quick, Bristol

repro   Twenty Twenty Displays, Falmouth

print   Triangle, Leeds

acknowledgements
Julie Roberts would like to thank The Public
Records Office at Kew for the research material for
Jack, and the Barbara Hepworth Estate for copyright
permission for the *Barbara Hepworth Wallpaper,*
which was designed by Timorous Beasties,
Glasgow, and printed at The Archive Printing
Company Limited, North Wales